A Honeymoon Voyage

A Journal of a Voyage on the ss Great Britain

Mary Crompton, just married and aged 20 years, wrote her journal onboard the ss Great Britain on the return voyage from Melbourne, Victoria, to Liverpool, England from May to July, 1866.

She was a remarkable lady; when most of the other passengers, including her husband, were sprawled in their bunks with sea-sickness she was enjoying her food, walking on deck and observing the waves, torn up by the wind and gales, and noting the progress of the ship. The Captain encouraged her to organise the singing and entertainment and each day she wrote an interesting account of incidents and life onboard.

Front and rear cover feature photographs of Mary Crompton at age 25 (approximately) and 85 respectively

BRUNEL'S
ss GREAT BRITAIN™

Published by ss Great Britain 2003-2011
Great Western Dockyard, Bristol BS1 6TY

www.ssgreatbritain.org
ISBN 9780951981404

Design, cover & layout by Keith Stanton 2011
Additional editing and copy by Flora Ocsag and Cathy Wrigley

Photographs by Keith Stanton, David Noton, Simon Dowling and Jo Baker

FOREWORD

BY KEITH STANTON

It has been many years since this book was originally published, and much has changed for the ss Great Britain during this time. Since the involvement of the original editor of this book, the late Peter Ward in 1992, Brunel's ss Great Britain has become one of Europe's leading visitor attractions, and in 2010 the site became home to The Brunel Institute, comprising a conservation suite, archive, a major reference library, and in addition the National Brunel Archive, the world's finest collection of original Brunel sources.

Brunel's ss Great Britain is now on permanent display for visitors every day of the year (apart from Christmas Eve and Christmas Day) and now sees over a hundred and fifty thousand visitors every year. It is situated in the very dry dock in which it was built in Bristol, England, over a hundred and sixty years ago.

The fascinating insights in this diary extract give just a small indication of what life must have been like for the passengers on the ss Great Britain during its many voyages, and an idea of life in Victorian times.

The diary extracts themselves have been edited by James Crompton (Mary's great grandson) and annotated throughout with reference numbers which are listed under 'Notes' on the back page. Please note that anything in italics, such as '*(sic)*' which incidentally means '*as written*', have been made by James Crompton to help with the continuity and understanding of the text.

Keith Stanton
Brunel's ss Great Britain 2011

Brunel's ss Great Britain in her original dry dock in Bristol today

PREFACE

BY PETER WARD

STEAM SHIP GREAT BRITAIN
HONI SOIT QUI MAL Y PENCE
DIEU ET MON DROIT

My purpose in writing this preface is threefold; First I should like to introduce James Crompton who carried out the research and edited the voyage journal of his Great grandmother, Susan Mary Crompton (née Clark); Secondly I feel that a word of explanation is in order to demonstrate the build standard of ss Great Britain. Major repair and reconstruction was required to enable the ship to win supremacy on the Australian run, which was to prove so successful in the years of 1860 to 1876. Thirdly, the map illustrations and drawings which accompany the text of journal, have been made possible by comparing Mary Crompton's remarks with previously published references of other voyages by the ss Great Britain to and from Australia.

ss Great Britain on the River Mersey in 1861
Painting courtesy of the Library of New South Wales

James Crompton. I first met James in 1960 when he had just returned to his home town of Adelaide, South Australia, to take up an appointment as a Radar scientist joining a newly formed Naval project group. Together with the other gifted entrepreneurs he worked at Weapons Research Establishment, South Australia, undertaking trials at Woomera and visits overseas.

Since the date we have become close personal friends and, when I suggested to him recently that his ancestors may have emigrated in ss Great Britain, he replied that, not only had his great grandfather, Joseph Crompton, emigrated on Voyage 19 in 1860, but 6 years later he had married Susan Mary Clark and together, they had returned to England in Voyage 28 in 1866 on a business and honeymoon trip. Mary had written a journal of her voyage which, although lodged with the project, had not previously been published. During a visit to England last year, James undertook to do further research and to edit the journal. I was commissioned to provide a foreword with appropriate illustrations to accompany the text. So here it is!

When Joseph Crompton emigrated in 1860, his parents had recently died, and together with his letter of introduction to the Clark family, he carried also an inheritance which enabled him to start up in business as a property owner. He obviously made rapid progress to be in a position to marry Mary and return to England in 1866. They travelled First Class and sat at the Captain's table. Mary described their cabins being on the Starboard side. This information, coupled with a study of the drawings given in Dr. Ewan Corlett`s book 'The Iron Ship' enables me to pinpoint the cabin as being one of three adjoining the Poop deck saloon.

Mary's photograph, appearing at the frontispiece of this book was taken several years after they had returned to Australia. The photograph at the end of the book shows Mary, aged 85, in December, 1931.

James Crompton's grandfather was born in Adelaide shortly after Joseph and Mary's return. Altogether Joseph and Mary had a family of eleven children.

ss Great Britain – Build Standard. Following the disastrous grounding of the ship in Dundrum Bay, Northern Ireland in 1846, she remained idle in Liverpool for several years awaiting repairs and a buyer. Fortunately, gold had just been discovered in Australia and trade was booming, so the new owners Gibbs and Bright, having Bristol and Liverpool connections, embarked on a programme of reconstruction. New machinery was installed, the cargo spaces were extended and an entirely new deckhouse was built to provide for passengers accommodation.

ss Great Britain at anchor in 1866

In a series of refits completed in 1853, 1855 and 1857, representing build standards, the whole concept of the sailing and steaming plan was altered. This meant that, for the main sequence of the Australian run, the ship had now become a very large sailing ship with auxiliary steam power instead of the original concept of a steamship with auxiliary sails.

ss Great Britain was now a very strong ship with three square rigged masts, a single funnel and a new lifting propeller. The propeller was two bladed which could be lifted out of the water–flow into a trunk just below the poop deck. In her journal, Mary describes this is a very noisy operation, but with a strong following wind, as in the Howling Fifties of the South Pacific, the ship could sail at a speed of 14 knots and a daily distance of some 300 miles.

Under steam alone, the speed was reduced to about 9 knots; with an adverse wind as in the North–East trades the first class passengers, aft of the funnel, became covered in black soot spots!

The Map Illustrations. The map illustrations which accompany Mary's journal are an amalgam of her remarks concerning each day's progress compared with Ewan Corlett's analysis of the route from his book 'The Iron Ship'. Also Adrian Ball, in his book 'Is Yours an ss Great Britain Family?' comments on the routes taken as follows:

> *"...Henceforth, she was destined to follow sailing ship routes, utilising the most favourable at all times. This normally meant sailing out around the Cape of Good Hope and home around Cape Horn ... Some of the most interesting and significant information on the voyages in those years come from the diaries, letters and ship's newspapers produced by the passengers. Thus we know that during Voyage 18 (March to May, 1860) Great Britain was under sail alone for 52.8 percent of the time, combined steam and sail for 31.7 percent, and solely steam for 15.5 per cent."*

Further information is given in the voyage account 'The Albatross', edited by Colonel Sir James E.A. Alexander, K.L.C.S., published in 1863. In this book, Captain Gray (who signed himself 'Lieut. R.N.R Commander ss Great Britain') wrote formally to the passengers each week with a copy of the Ship's daily log. Thus we have the most detailed and authoritative account of the route taken. This I have compared with Mary's own detailed remarks to compile a curved idealistic route showing the ship's approximate position on each day of the voyage. One point of the departure from that given in Ewan Corlett's account is that on crossing the Equator on about 30 degree meridian, she then veered to a Westerly course passing West of the Azores and approaching the coast of Ireland from a South–Westerly direction.

Peter Ward
Member of the ss Great Britain Project

A Voyage on the Great Britain

Extracts of the Journal of Susan Mary Crompton

Annotated By James Crompton

1854.
THURSDAY, 19.
FRIDAY, 20.
SATURDAY, 21.

"Great Britain" May 15th 1866

I do not mean to keep a regular journal, for I think a ship journal is a very disagreeable thing to keep and very tiresome to read afterwards…

These are the first words in a green octavo notebook which came into my care some years ago. They were written by my great grandmother, Susan Mary Crompton (Mary to her family), soon after sailing from Melbourne with her young husband Joseph in May, 1866, bound for Liverpool around Cape Horn.

Mary's parents, Francis and Caroline Clark, had emigrated from Birmingham and settled with their family in South Australia when she was four years old. Born in 1846, she was the youngest of their eleven children, three of whom have died young from lung diseases aggravated by the atmospheric pollutions of the 19th century industrial England.

The last victim was their Son Francis, who, before he died in 1849 aged 21, implored his parents to take his surviving brothers and sisters to a healthier climate. It was the advice of Caroline's elder brother, Rowland Hill of Penny Postage fame, who had been Secretary to the South Australian Commissioners at the time of founding of the colony, that led them to arrive in Adelaide in 1850.

Joseph Crompton, my great grandfather, emigrated in the Great Britain from Liverpool in 1860 and bringing with him a letter of introduction to the Clarks. He settled in Adelaide and married Mary early in 1866.

Their voyage in the Great Britain was, no doubt, partly honeymoon and partly business. Here and there the journal has erasures and corrections initialled "J.C." Although only six years her senior, his relationship with his young bride seems to have been remarkably paternal!

Luggage on the dockside at Brunel's ss Great Britain

Departure

To embark on the Great Britain for the long voyage to Liverpool, Mary and Joseph had first to travel from Adelaide to Melbourne in a small coastal sailing ship named Coorong. Great Britain was apparently anchored off-shore in Port Phillip Bay being, too large to be taken up the River Yarra to Port Melbourne. Mary's journal begins:

"May 15. We came on board with Sidney *(one of her brothers)* late on the afternoon ... We had some difficulty for there were numbers of boats crowding round the staircase and the men were roaring at one another and pushing about till I thought we should all be in the water. There were numbers of people about who had come to wish their friends goodbye and these filled every corner of the ship till one could hardly stir.

Typical First Class Cabin onboard the ss Great Britain

We found Mrs. Sinnott who had very kindly come to see us off, she was alone and had been hustled about by the crowd for an hour before we came. After dinner she went on shore with Sidney who however came to bid us goodbye. I did not like his going. I am afraid I had a cry but Joe is very kind and he soon made me feel happy again. He is very good to me, he never leaves me for long and when he is amusing himself elsewhere he comes every now and then to see if I'm happy."

ss Great Britain Promenade Deck

At Sea

"May 16. We started about 8 o'clock a.m. and steamed slowly down the Bay. It was calm beautiful day the ship hardly rolled; we spent most of our time putting our cabin in order. It is a comfortable little place about 9ft by 6ft. Here is a plan. I can't draw straight lines the ship rolls so.

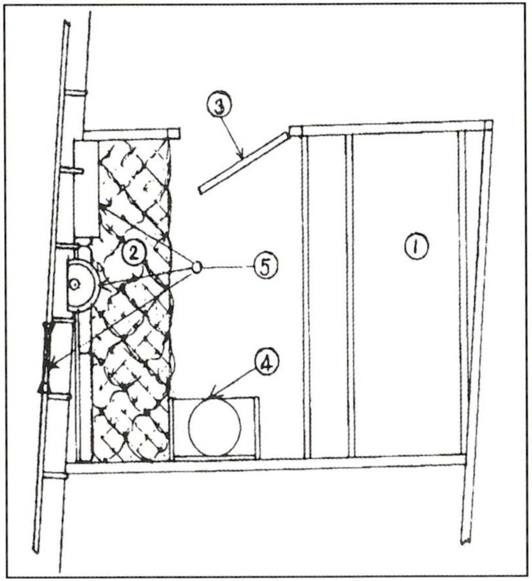

Plan of Joe and Mary's cabin

1. Bunk beds. Lower berth widened. Upper berth used only for stowage.

2. Padded sofa.

3. Door.

4. Washstand.

5. Shelf, candlelamp and Porthole (starboard side).

No.1 is the berth. Joe has had the lower one enlarged and we only use the top one to keep things in, such as our warm rugs, coats, dresses, bandbox etc. No.2 is a sofa all nicely padded, over it a shelf with a ledge where we keep all our books, and a candle lamp is fixed to the side of the cabin. No.3 is the door which opens into a little passage; No. 4 is the washstand, between it and the bed we have placed one of my boxes which serves as a seat, all the rest of our baggage is put under the berth and sofa firmly cleated down."

Mary does not tell us that the Captain (Note 1) was the same as on Joe's Voyage in 1860. However, Reference 1 states that John Gray was the ship's captain from 1854 until he was lost at sea in 1872. She does say that she felt "highly honoured by the Captain putting us at his table.".

Portrait of Captain John Gray

"The saloon is very large. There are 6 tables, all covered with red cloths with long seats on each side padded with crimson velvet; the walls are painted in small pannels *(sic)* with the arms of different countries, and a mirror between each pannel. Over the table are long wooden stands with holes fitted with wineglasses and decanters; the woodwork in the room is painted like maple, altogether it's a bright looking room.

I don't sit in it much except at meal times and for short time in the evenings; it is very draughty and people will sit there with their hats on and it provokes me. There are 90 saloon passengers and my impression is that they are a queer lot, one old woman comes to meals with her bonnet on, I wonder if she goes to bed with it, I've never seen her without *(it)* yet. At present everyone is so sea-sick that I do not know much about them yet but from their looks I think I shall have very little to do with most of them.

Mr Fenwick sits next to me at table and seems disposed to be pleasant, he is a grave gentlemanly man with a pretty wife *(Note 2)* who looks a good many years his junior, and two children of 8 and 9; his wife has not spoken to me, she is too sea-sick to know at present. The Farrar's are promising. Miss F. I think I shall like very much, she is plain and ladylike, seems very sensible and as if she worked very hard at home. I should think she was five or six years older than I am, she has a little brother and a crippled sister of 14 whom I have hardly seen. Mr Farrar, Dr Sanger and a Roman Catholic priest, who sits at the next table and looks very pleasant, get up a good deal of fun at table. There are swarms of children, I don't know whom they belong to; 24 in all.

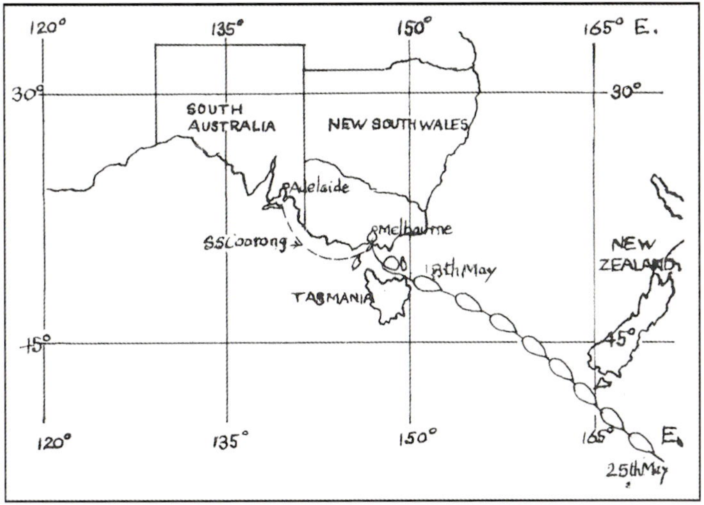

Grand Departure of ss Great Britain. Voyage No. 28 - 15th May 1886

May 17, their first full day at sea, "was rather rough, the wind was dead against us and so strong that we could hardly make our way, it was a wild night the captain did not go to bed, we were knocking about trying to go through Bass's *(Note 3)* straits but it was no use, we were beaten out of our course and the Captain was so much afraid of the rocks about us that we had to turn and go straight back till morning."

"May 18 was very rough. I was the only lady at breakfast, there was only one beside myself at lunch. I felt rather green but I was not at all seasick. Poor Joe was miserably sick. He was lying down a great part of the day and I put him to bed directly after dinner, we had the dead lights up *(Note 4)* and passed a dismal day.

When it is rough I lie awake half the night; I suppose I shall get used to the noises but I never heard anything like them before; it is really dreadful when they take up the screw; the men seem to drag great chains along the decks just over our heads for about half an hour banging them down at intervals."

"May 19 Much calmer, yesterday I could not understand how anybody could endure being at sea, today I think it is very pleasant.

The Poop Deck Dining Saloon

This ship was forced to go so completely out of her course that we have lost two days. I heard Mr O`Shannasy tell Captain Grey *(sic)* that he would have given him £50 more passage money if he would have waited a day longer at Melbourne. The Captain said he wished he had for the bad weather had cost him £100. He came down to breakfast this morning the first meal he has taken with us since the rough weather began, he has been so anxious and busy that his passengers have seen very little of him yet."

"They keep a magnificent table on board everything is very nice except the bread, butter, tea and coffee; we have rolls at breakfast which are very well made. I never saw such a place as this for eating, people seem to do very little else. We have breakfast at 9, lunch at 12, dinner at 4 and tea at 7:30 o'clock, the children have their meals at different times from the grown up people, so the stewards seem to be doing nothing all day but laying or clearing tables.

We have 12 stewards to wait at dinner, 2 for each table, it is very funny to watch them bringing in the dishes; one rings a little bell which is the signal for the cook to send things up from the lower regions, then the 12 stand in a row down the saloon passing the dishes like fireman pass buckets; on rough days they have to stand slanting and look very comical, they very seldom drop the things; one split a cup of tea down a gentleman's back yesterday. Lunch is the pleasantest meal of the day, we have hot soup, cold meat, bread and cheese."

"Sunday May 20. We had service in the saloon at half past ten conducted by a dreadful old stick of a clergyman. I shall not like to stay away from the service but really he will be an infliction before we come to the end of our voyage. He reads very very badly with a nasal twang, a sing song manner and a peculiar habit of raising his voice at the end of each sentence. He read the church service for the morning Dr Sanger officiating as clerk. Then he preached a dismal sermon about Shadrach Mishach and Abednego beginning with a few laudatory remarks about the captain and passengers, I felt quite sorry for the captain. There is a Presbyterian minister on board, a pleasant looking elderly gentleman. I believe he will conduct the other. We had no singing last Sunday, the captain wishes us to have some, he asked me to help so I am glad I brought my little tune book. It did not seem at all like Sunday. I was glad when the day was over."

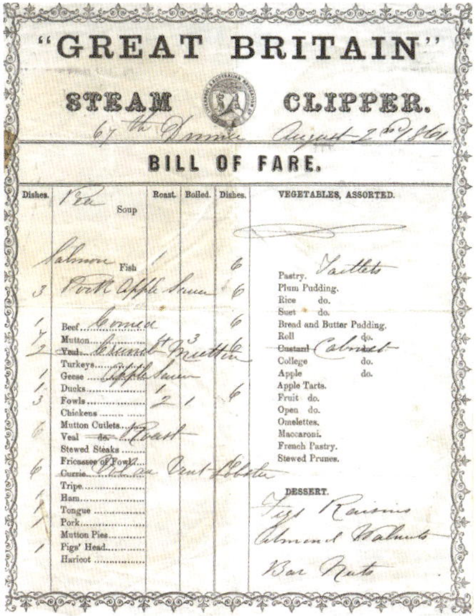
"GREAT BRITAIN"
STEAM CLIPPER.
BILL OF FARE.

Dishes. Soup — Roast. Boiled. Dishes. — VEGETABLES, ASSORTED.

Fish

Beef, Mutton, Veal, Turkeys, Geese, Ducks, Fowls, Chickens, Mutton Cutlets, Veal do., Stewed Steaks, Fricassee of Fowl, Currie, Tripe, Ham, Tongue, Pork, Mutton Pies, Pigs' Head, Haricot

Pastry. Plum Pudding. Rice do. Suet do. Bread and Butter Pudding. Roll do. Custard College do. Apple do. Apple Tarts. Fruit do. Open do. Omelettes. Maccaroni. French Pastry. Stewed Prunes.

DESSERT.

Sample Menu from 1861

The Dining Saloon reconstructed as it was in 1843

"May 21. We did a most disgraceful thing this morning. The last few nights have been so noisy that we are very short of sleep and today we did not even wake up till the breakfast bell rang at 9 o'clock, we dressed as fast as we could but breakfast was so nearly over that we were ashamed *(note 5)* to go in and made an impromptu meal off *(sic)* biscuits and Fred's dried figs. Just now we are having very foggy weather so I do not go on deck much. Joe, Mr Farrar, Dr Sanger and the captain play at whist sometimes for 3d. points."

"May 22. Very damp and foggy. I am astonished that we feel the cold so little; the captain says it will not be much colder but we don't believe it. Joe has put up a nice little table that fits on to the wash-stand but we only put it in its place when we want it; we have made our cabin very comfortable and we sit in it most of the day when we are not on deck. There are more than 800 people on board of whom 700 are passengers. 8 stowaways have been found."

"May 23 .... I made friends with a young man from New Canterbury in New Zealand ..... He told me that he once met a Maouri *(sic)* lady well dressed in English clothes with a hat and veil over her mouth with a short black pipe sticking through it."

"Thursday May 24. It is a queer life here, it is pleasant enough but very unsatisfactory. I seem to get nothing done what we are eating and sleeping there is very little time for anything else. We are never up before 9 o'clock *(breakfast time)* it is very lazy but there is no use getting up, the deck is so wet one cannot walk, the saloon is very cold and the children are having their breakfast and it is not pleasant doing anything in our cabin till it has been aired, and we so often lie awake at night with rolling and the noises that we are glad of the time to sleep in the morning. I go on deck as soon as I can after breakfast to walk with Joe. I walk for an hour or two every day. The screw was taken up just before lunch time so we stayed on deck to watch the operation. After dinner some of us went into the ladies saloon and had some music. Mr Murray sang some pretty Scotch song, he sings very well, Jane accompanied him and played some pieces, I was singing too. The piano is a good one in a very fair tune. I don't go too often, I am afraid of troubling people, and I am afraid too lest any of my horrors should come to listen: there is one or two men on board I would not speak to for anything. One of them is a great coward, he has nightmares and lies screaming that the ship is sinking much to the disturbance of his neighbours.

I had some games of backgammon with the captain. I have not joined in any whist or chess, no one that I know plays chess and I have not had a rubber *(best of three games)* because the gentleman Joe plays with always plays for three–penny points and I don't like to play for money. What a very nice man the captain is, he seems always to be looking out for something to make his passengers more comfortable, he generally chooses those ladies who are travelling alone to walk with. Among so many of course he cannot give much time to each one but he always has a pleasant word or smile for everyone. I think he was pleased at receiving Emily's letter, he has spoken of her many times.

He has found out a poor little boy of 9 years old in a second cabin who does not know a soul on board, his father who has married a second wife is sending him to some friends in England.

The wind is very unsatisfactory, it blows well for a day or so then either dies away or blows against us and the captain is afraid to use the screw any more then can be helped lest the coal should not last."

Promenade Deck

"Friday, May 25 was the coldest day we have had. I spent a great part of my time coiled up in our possum rug, it is so warm. Joe makes me take such brisk walks that I don't feel the cold so much as I should do if I was lazy. Mrs. Fenwick *(who plays very well and sings pretty well)*, Miss Carrington, Dr Sanger and I practised some hymns from Sunday in parts as the captain wished it."

"Saturday poor Jane is in bed with a bad cold and headache. I read to her all the evening."

"Sunday, May 27 was such a beautiful day and much warmer. We had again to listen to that dreadful stick – he went through the service better, but the sermon was if possible more milk and watery then last Sunday's. Our hymns were satisfactory. I read to Jane after tea and spent the rest of the evening with Miss Farrar and Joe in the ladies saloon playing and singing; it was much more like a Sunday at last. I am very happy all day but sometimes in the evening I get very homesick. I suppose I shall get used to being away in time."

"Monday *(May 28)* is a nice day very bright and sunny; we are going to have another Monday tomorrow .... I was walking with the captain the other day and I asked him if he was not very proud of his ship. "Dear little girl", he exclaimed. "I love every plank of her. I pat her sometimes and I've promised her a rest if she will only get home in less than 70 days." There is such an odd looking young man on board. He is tall, lanky with brilliant red hair and whiskers and he always wears a sky blue felt hat, at meal times as well as on deck; when he walks he looks as though he had borrowed somebody else's legs for the day and was going out to try them.

Do you remember about 12 years ago a vessel called the Madagascar leaving Melbourne that was never heard of; people now know what became of her. Some time ago a man was arrested for an attempt to seize a vessel on the way from Melbourne to England. He was sent as a convict to Malta and he then confessed that he was on board the Madagascar and that he had organised an insurrection: those of the crew who would not help him, the captain and all the passengers were murdered; the ship was run on shore on the South American coast and he and his accomplices stole all the gold. Was it not an awful business? The Farrars had some friends on board."

Entertainments

"Monday, May 28th No.2. *(having crossed the International Dateline)*. It feels strange to have this day as if we were taking what did not belong to us or turning nature upside down to suit our purposes.

We had a general meeting in the saloon to consider how we might amuse ourselves during the voyage; it was resolved that if possible one evening every week some of us should combine to entertain the others with music, reading, etc. A concert was arranged for Wednesday; a committee of 12 was chosen and a select committee consisting of Mrs Fenwick, Dr Sanger and myself to arrange the evening's programme. My fellow workers have several glees with them so we three, a Mr Crebach and Miss Carrington set about learning some of them; as they are new to me I find it rather hard work learning 3 in so short a time.

First Class passengers socialising on the Promenade Deck

Dr Sanger is that very queer looking old man that Effie saw on board the Coorong .... I don't much admire him but he has a good voice, sings a comic song with great spirit and has a capital notion of keeping people in order while singing. He beats time furiously and snaps us up shortly if anyone makes a mistake. I am so much amused at him that I don't mind his sharp words but I do not like him calling Mrs Fenwick to account though I think she does not mind. Miss Carrington sings well, much better than she plays, Mr Crebach is not much account. I am teaching Miss Farrar to play backgammon. We have a rubber of games every evening."

"Wednesday *(May 30)* A breeze sprang up yesterday that was freshening all night. At 12 o'clock today we had gone 312 miles our longest distance; we are racing along so fast the great waves can't catch us, one however came over the deck and soaked several of the gentleman. I think I was the only lady who went on deck all day; the sea looked beautiful, it is the first time I have seen really large waves, as we stood near the wheel we saw many come to the ship that rose above the horizon, great black fellows that raced after us tumbling over one another and breaking into sheets of white foam.

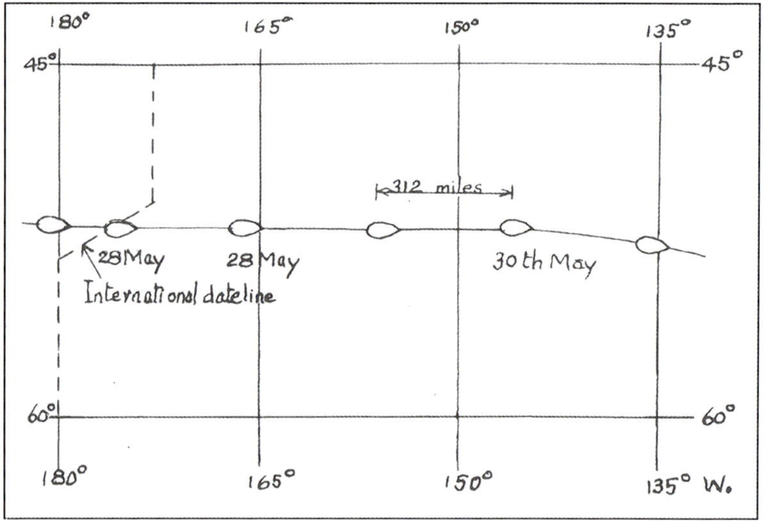

Entertainments across the Pacific Ocean

I saw some stormy petrels but except for a few Cape pidgeons *(sic)* the wind has driven away all our birds. The weather was so rough we could not have our concert. I have felt so strong and well since we left home much better than I have done for a a long time not that there was anything the matter with me then, but expecting a very little toothache, I am so particularly comfortable; I have not even chilblains. We have the deadlights down."

"Thursday *(May 31)* still rough, our cabin is so dark now it is shut up. A great wave came yesterday and wet all the cabins on our side of the ship, fortunately I was just out of bed and had shut the window and as fast as the water came in I mopped it up with towels so we did not get much wet, but in Mrs O`Shannasey`s cabin the window was open and the water poured in washing backwards and forwards over the floor soaking everything."

"Saturday *(June 2)* We have gone over 900 miles in the last three days. I don't tell the distances generally, it is commonly over 200, but our shortest run was 103 miles. We are doing as much without the crew as possible for Captain Gray is afraid of using the coal too fast. We had our concert this evening at 8 o'clock, the piano was moved into the saloon for the purpose; this was our programme:

Overture	Fra Diavola	Mrs Crompton
Glee	O who will o`er the downs	
Solo	Sweet spirit hear my prayer	Mrs. Fenwick
Duett	Home to our mountains	Mrs. C. and Miss Carrington
	Mazurka	Mrs. Fenwick
Song		Dr Sanger
Glee	Viva Enrico	
	Interval of ship`s band	
Glee	Blow gentle gales	
Solo Piano	Carnival de Venise	Miss Carrington
Duett	Flow gently Diva	Mrs. Fenwick
		Dr Sanger
Solo	The Auld House	Mr. Murray
Solo Piano	O dear What can the Matter be	Miss *(name illegible)*
Solo Comic	Mrs Parrington's advice to singers	Dr Stanger
Solo Duett and chorus	God Save the Queen"	

Mrs Fenwick, Miss Carrington, Dr Sanger, Mr Crebach and myself sang the glees. I think it went off well the people were pleased, they encored "Viva Enrico" a lively Italian song; the performance lasted about an hour and a half."

"Sunday, June 3rd. The captain took Joe and me into his cabin one day, and into the cook's galley and the second class saloon, he says he will take me all over the ship when the weather is warmer. He has two cabins, a sitting room and bed-room, he has everything so comfortable .... The engineer often comes to dinner but none of the mates ever come: Mr Peterson heard of the death of his wife only a few days before we sailed and I think for that reason he mixes very little with the passengers: he is the first officer, the second is Mr. Todhunter, they are both pleasant looking men.

Drawing of the Poop Deck by Melbourne passenger Herman Zumpstein, 1863

Icebergs and Gales

"Wednesday *(June 6)* We saw two icebergs, the only ones we have sighted, they were small perhaps 150 ft. high, they were very like what my fancy painted. The one on the port side was a chill blue very like a cloud with sharply defined edges, that on the starboard side was a clear white with the shadows the most delicate cobalt blue, the light was on it and it did indeed look beautiful. I tried to paint it out of our cabin window but it is funny production …

We have been a good deal provoked by Mrs O'Shannasey bringing some rough Irishmen to our table every evening to play at a noisy gambling game of cards, our own gentlemen occupied the other end of the table playing at whist so we ladies were forced to spend the evenings in our own cabins or go to one of the other tables; the captain was very indignant about it but did not want to speak himself because it would have created so much ill feeling, but he told Mr Farrar and me not stir for anybody, we did so and got Mrs. Fenwick to join us and we spent a very merry evening playing at games."

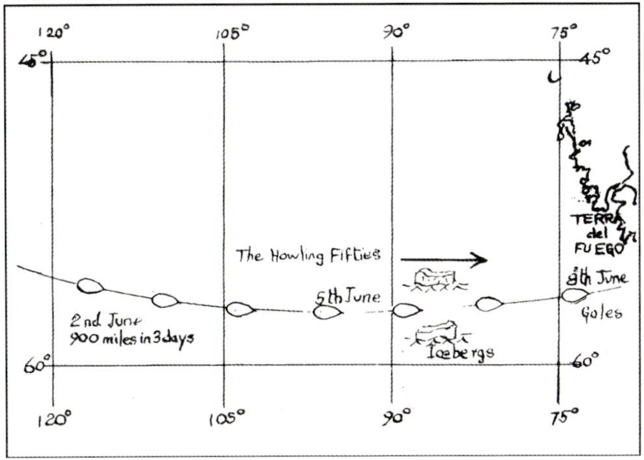

Sailing before the wind; large waves and gales

"Friday *(June 8)* During dinner a storm sprang up. The captain ran up on deck and we never saw him again that evening, there was a tremendous noise on deck and the ship rolled so; I was too much amused at the way people and things tumbled about to feel frightened, the gale continued all night, but it did us no harm beyond breaking a chain: the wind was so high that the sailors were trying to reef a sail for 4 hours before they succeeded."

Saturday *(June 9)* The gale has subsided, the sun was shining brightly and the sea was glorious; even the captain said it was very high it reminded me of a view over the ranges at home, hills beyond hills as far as the eyes could reach; the great waves came tearing along behind us in huge walls of water high above the deck and looking as if they must sink us, but we flew before the wind and they could not catch us. Those beautiful waves, I never saw anything like them before, such brilliant colours, blue and black and green and everywhere streaked and crested with snowy mountains of foam."

ss Great Britain sailing through icebergs

Births and Deaths…

"Sunday *(June 10)* I forgot to say we passed the Horn about 10 o'clock yesterday morning 25 days out: it has put people in spirits …. During the night one of the saloon passengers, a Mrs Moses had a baby but it was born dead; the poor woman has been ill ever since we sailed, she has one little girl though she is only just 20."

"Tuesday *(June 12)* Last night a child was born in the steerage and a poor old man died, he was upwards of 80 and had none of his relations on board with him; was buried early this morning.

ss Great Britain rounding Cape Horn

Illustration by George Cruikshank of Bombastes Furioso -
one of the many plays on Mary's journey

… and more Entertainments

The charade came off this evening; the captain had a curtain made of flags put up and a pretty painted drop scene. The word was 'wilful', the first scene discovered Joe and Miss Tabatha Peticoat and her nephew *(Mr Alfrey)*; her brother having lately died.

Dr Sanger as an old lawyer assisted by Mr. Leonard Fosbury as clerk read the will and a very funny will it was. Among other things the old man had left behind him in his museum: the spout of the great Khan of Tartary.

The property was left to his two sons, the eldest, Doughboy *(Mr Alfrey)*, went to Australia, the youngest, Toby *(Mr O'Shannasey)* was left under the care of his aunt.

In the second scene, Doughboy having spent all of his money comes home in the roughest clothes and does all he can to shock his aunt; in the last scene the wilful boy Toby appeared and after a little talking they all danced a jig. Joe and Mr O'S. did look so funny, we borrowed some of Miss Farrar's clothes for Joe, her things were just the right length, then he had my crinoline and we borrowed a cap to hide his whiskers; he made a splendid old maid.

You can imagine Mr O'S. was a comical sight when I tell you that he was dressed in a short chintz petticoat and a white garibaldi trimmed with red and trowsers to match and he is 6ft. 3 or 4 and broad in proportion: we made his waistband 54in, according to Captain Fosbury's measurement. He came in drawing a child's cart and blowing a tin trumpet.

Volunteer Ron Bloomfield playing piano on the ss Great Britain

Heading North into the Tropics

"Thursday, June 14 is a beautiful day, it is such a pleasure to see the sun and feel it getting warmer; when we have seen it before it had such an idiotic look just above the horizon in the middle of the day. Lately we have not been able to do anything after half past three; 57'58' is our lowest latitude. We had games again in the evening, the captain joined us and we had great fun.

Some time ago the carpenter had a bad accident, one of the large pieces of beef that was tied high up the mast fell upon him; he was not much hurt but he has been ill some time in consequence; he is better now."

"Sunday, June 17th Mr Conabee preached, he had not arranged the hymns with anyone, so Mr Murray and Dr Sanger each waited for the other to begin, when up jumped three men from the second saloon and began to sing a most dismal tune very slowly; they quite took the responsibility of the music and they chose tunes that did not suit the hymns. When they came to the last word there were half a dozen notes to spare."

"Wednesday *(June 20)* It is getting warmer fast, we are beginning to grumble at the heat now; there is a horrible headwind that has blown since the last Saty *(sic)*. We are getting on very slowly though we use 45 tons of coal a day: we are only going 150 or 180 miles."

"Thursday *(June 21)* was a miserable day, the wind blew all the smoke over the deck till the blacks *(Note 7)* lay in drifts; our cabin was strewn with them, but it is the first time they have troubled us."

"Sunday, June 24. A perfectly delightful day, it positively felt like Sunday; the sea was quite calm and sometimes a great black fish swam by some 20 feet long. We had a *(Church of England)* service on deck. Mr King preached and we sang several hymns and chants *(Note 8)*. The Roman Catholics had their service at nine, we began at half past ten, and Mr Conabee held a *(Presbyterian)* service at half past two, the captain attended all three so he had enough of it.

The quarter master came out in their clean white dresses and blue collars, and the officers broke out in buttons: we had quite a muster of them at dinner, the engineer and the first and second mates all came. I like Mr Todhunter very much, I had a long talk with him that evening; he was once the captain of the ship, but she was wrecked through no fault of his and the Trinity board suspended his certificate for a year and he said it had ruined him.

We have a moon now and it is so delightful I spend most of the evenings on deck, the nights are perfectly glorious.

We are beginning to see the rats, one came into my cabin the other night as I was going to bed, I jumped onto the berth and waited till Joe came down, then he and one of the stewards had a grand rat hunt but the gentleman escaped through the hole. Mrs Fenwick was wakened by one biting her toe nails, and Jane Cumming has had a new stocking eaten by another."

"Monday, *(June 25)* Two of the stewards had a fight in the pantry. One of them is to stay in the steerage and have his pay stopped for the rest of the voyage as a punishment. We had a dance on the deck in the moonlight, it was very pleasant, the band played for us but very few of the passengers would join. There was another little baby born; Mrs Austin's baby has been so ill I was afraid it would die, but it has taken a turn for the better ... I think we are very fortunate in having so quiet a set of passengers; two widows had a great quarrel last week, but that is almost the only disturbance we have had. Joe saw the first flying fish yesterday."

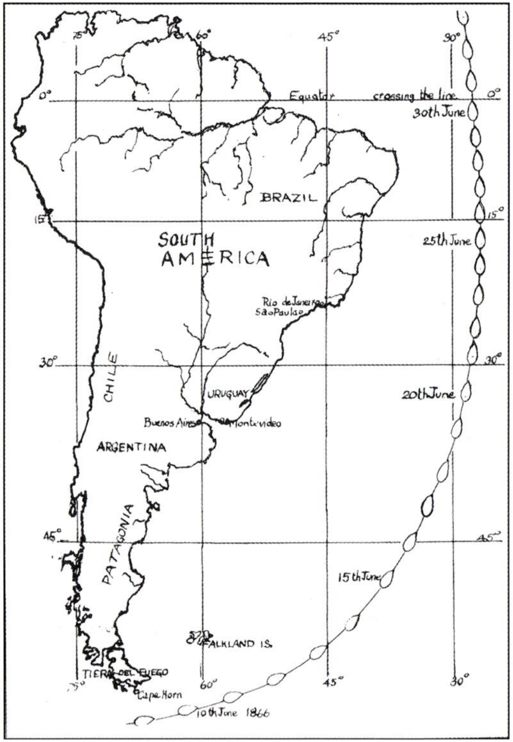

Heading north into the Tropics

"Wednesday, *(June 27)* We had some more dancing and enjoyed it much more than the last, a great many more joined .... the ship was steady but she lay over on one side and the dancers were continually losing their balance and sitting down on the skylight unintentionally."

"Thursday *(June 28)* We gave a concert on deck in the evening, it went off very well; we sang several glees, of course without any accompaniment the band played and some of us sang solos, myself among the number. We had a very large audience, I suppose 5 or 600."

"Saturday *(June 30)* Still the most beautiful weather in the evening we played at proverbs etc., on deck. Crossed the line in the night."

"Sunday, July 1st. After lunch the captain took Miss Carrington, Mrs Murray and myself over part of the ship; we first went to the storeroom to be weighed. I am 8 stone 13lb ... and the captain 16st 10lb., then we explored the 2nd class saloon and cabins, the steerage and intermediate; the ship is very well ventilated, but the people are packed as close as bees in a hive: in the steerage where the people pay only £16 passage money there are 8 in each cabin. 4 berth on each side with a narrow passage between and the washstand. I saw one little child sitting up in bed playing with a cullender *(sic)*.

Wherever we went the captain was sure to roar at someone for staying downstairs, and everyone looked so pleased, they all love him. I should like to go into the engine room but the stairs or rather ladder are in such a narrow place I don`t like to venture.

On Saturday night two ships passed us and today, Monday, we have seen 4 more; we spoke *(to)* one, it was such fun talking to her; she said she was a Prussian vessel named the "Ferdinand Brunn", she was 32 days out from Sunderland and was bound for Singapore.

Steerage onboard the ss Great Britain

Another little baby born this morning, and Mrs Austin`s poor baby died about 10 o`clock, she has been very ill all this last week and early this morning she was seized with convulsions which continued till she died: she was a nice little thing of 5 month old, with long curly brown hair, I never saw a child with so much at her age."

"Tuesday *(July 3)* Just after dinner a small brig passed us so close we could have thrown something into her, our captain climbed into one of the boats and had a conversation with her captain. She was such a little bit of a thing, there seems to be only about dozen men on board, she was bound for Rio. The second class gave a concert on deck, it was much too long and very dreary collection of songs. Very hot all day."

"Wednesday *(July 4)* Much cooler, we have done with the severe heat which has only lasted 3 days; either we have had a singularly fortunate passage or people grumble far too much at the heat and cold."

"Friday *(July 6)* We had another concert on deck, really I should think there was a ship full of persevering musical talent."

"Saturday, *(July 7)* We passed a French vessel and spoke *(to)* her with flags, she was an ugly tub and we passed her in no time though we were only sailing. The weather is perfectly delightful. We are out of the tropics now."

"Tuesday *(July 10)* Dr Sanger is getting up "Bombastes Furiso". I take the part of Disdaffena; we are very busy with rehearsals every day. We had dancing on deck all the evening and enjoyed it greatly; it was the pleasantest we have had: there are several good dancers among our numerous young men and most of them I like very much. Leonard Fosbery got a teapot full of champagne for us after we left off dancing: then we had Miss Farrar and Mr. Allfrey to a biscuit and cheese supper in our cabin."

"Wednesday *(July 11)* Joe is very busy getting up a charade for next Monday, it is a kind of hash of "Domestic Broils". During dinner we had a disturbance, two of the stewards had a fight outside the door of the saloon, the captain jumped up and soon stopped *(it)* by hitting at each of them."

Thursday *(July 12)* Last night a poor man was lost, he was seen about 12 o`clock but no–one knows anything of him since, it is supposed that he jumped overboard; he has been very quiet and melancholy ever since we sailed; he was a German in the steerage. A woman belonging to the second cabin had twins.

We had the burlesque of *"Bombastes Furioso"* in the evening, it went off very well. Dr Sanger was Bombastes, Mr Allfrey the king and Mr Fosbery *(was)* Fusbos; the dresses were very pretty, they were all borrowed from different people. We dressed like Turks. Mr O`Shannassey and a little man were the gallant army. The captain was pleased; he begins to laugh whenever he looks at me."

Replica calf's head, taken from a contemporary recipe book

A Wreck

"Saturday *(July 14)* There was great excitement about 11 o`clock. A cask half covered with seaweed passed us then people began to look about and we saw a wreck about three miles away. The captain said he was certain there was nobody on it, and he would have passed it by, but several of the passengers made a great fuss and thought they could see a man standing on the wreck, so to please them the captain said he would go to look; when we reached the place it was such a little bit of a thing I wonder we could see it so far away, it must have been there a long time as it was covered with barnacles: it was the shell of a small ship almost level with the water, every wave washing over it."

"Sunday, July 15th. Quite a cold day: three services on deck as normal but I did not go to any of them. We have not seen many rats lately but today they have been very troublesome, this evening I was by myself in the cabin so I began to read aloud to frighten them but one did not mind the noise and came close to me; I can't bear the creatures and the ship swarms with them."

"Monday *(July 16)* Very busy all day about our charade, it came off in the evening and I think the people liked it very much, the dresses were capital. After the charade was over the captain gave a grand supper, a purse of £50 was given to him some healths drunk and several votes of thanks passed, then we all sang 'God Save the Queen' and went to bed: it was rather dreary. The tables looked very pretty, there were numbers of little flags stuck in the dishes and figures made I think of wax placed here and there. Some of the joints were ornamented with little pieces of pink and white dough laid on in patterns; and two others were made to imitate ducks with tails and wings made of real feathers. There were also sponge cakes covered with pretty patterns in sugar and 'We are homeward bound' round the foot. There was a boar's head at the head of one table, I never saw one before and it was one of the nicest dishes I have tasted."

THE ILLUSTRATED LONDON NEWS.

No. 1685.—VOL. LIX. SATURDAY, DECEMBER 23, 1871. PRICE FIVEPENCE

London Illustrated News from 1871 showing a Boar's Head

An Accident

"Wednesday, *(July 18)* About 5 o'clock we had a very sad accident. A sailor *(one of the best on the ship)* was busy painting the anchor and in some way lost his footing and fell into the water first striking the anchor with his head ; a boat was lowered in a few minutes and soon found him lying on his back in the water,, his head bleeding frightfully; he was lifted by ropes to the deck and the doctors attended to him immediately, they found that his skull was fractured in two places and he had a deep cut over one ear besides. He has hitherto supported his old parents with his wages so a subscription has been got up for him. £50 has been collected of which the 2nd 3rd and 4th class passengers gave £32. The poor young man may get well but I am afraid there is not much chance."

A Victorian Penny - £50 would be equivalent to over £2000 today

Dockyard dressing at Brunel's ss Great Britain

Journey's end

"Thursday *(July 19)* We sighted Cape Clear about 7 a.m., the first land we have seen since we left Melbourne heads: how pleasant it is to see it once more. We spent most of the day on deck watching the Irish coast, it was rather hazy but we were often so near land we could see a great deal. It is very rocky but at the summit of the cliffs we could see many houses and corn fields and a few people. The most beautiful point we saw the Old Head of Kinsale it is a fine rock rising almost perpendicularly out of the water; on the summit there is a lighthouse painted red and white, with a low stone wall round it: we could see some people looking over it and waving their handkerchiefs; one was an old woman in a white cap. We saw the entrance to Cork Harbour where a large regatta was going on. We have so nearly run out of coals that the Captain thought we should be obliged to put into Queenstown for more *(but)* he finds it is not necessary. We saw a great many ships, twice there were 14 in sight."

"Friday, July 20th. We sighted the coast of Wales about 5 a.m. We watched it out of our cabin windows for some time then dressed and went on deck. It was a perfect morning, the sun was shining brightly, the sea lay calm and still, and the white sea gulls were flying about looking so pretty. We passed very near to Holyhead, it looked beautiful half hidden in the mist. We finished our packing and dined at 1 o'clock and then the bustle began, it really was dreadful: two steamers came up with numbers of men from the customs house who immediately set to work to carry the luggage on board. The ship was turned upside down, everybody got into a state of excitement and boxes kept coming up as if there was no end to them, to say nothing of bundles, bags, chairs and portmantoes *(sic)*. This confusion continued for some two hours and in the midst of it Mrs. Gray and the Captain's four little daughters came on board. The Captain introduced me to all of them; Mrs Gray is nice looking and the girls are all pretty, they are very different from the Australian children.

At last we got away in one of the steamers but it was a grief to leave the beautiful ship: the Captain stood on his bridge and gave a hearty cheer to which we responded again and again. Away we flew to the customs house where we had to sit for a long time while our luggage was brought in and examined; then we got a cab and a stout little horse which brought us and our luggage to South Hill Road."

Postscript

Mary and Joe returned to Adelaide in 1867 where my grandfather, the eldest of their eleven children, was born soon afterwards. Mary lived on well into living memory dying in 1932 aged 86. Her great grandchildren, at least, are grateful that she made a record of life in the 'Great Britain' and find it not in the least 'tiresome to read afterwards'. One of them, my cousin Alan Crompton, left a photo – copy of her Journal in Bristol when he visited 'Great Britain' in 1989. The original is now held in The Mortlock Library in Adelaide where it is accessible for historical research.

James Crompton, Adelaide, February 1992

NOTES:

(1)Reference 1 provides, inter alia, the following information about the Captain:
"John Gray ... took command on 20 April (1854). A Shetlander, he was a forceful man ... and excelled both at getting on with the passengers and at taking command at times of stress. As is often the case, much of the success of a ship in her subsequent career depends upon her master and she was well served by John Gray."
(2)The word "pretty" has been struck out in pencil – by Joe apparently!
(3)Bass`s" has been struck out by Joe and "Banks" inserted in his hand. Banks Strait lies between the Furneaux Group and the north – east tip of Tasmania. Apparently the Captain had hoped to pass through it thereby keeping as close as possible to the great circle route to Cape Horn.
(4)"up" struck out and "down" inserted in Joe`s hand.
(5)"bosh J.C." inserted over "ashamed"!
(6)Emily was the eldest of the Clark family and some twenty years Mary`s senior. She broke off an engagement in 1850 to accompany her parents to South Australia. She never saw her fiancé again and died unmarried in 1911.
(7)The Concise Oxford Dictionary, which Mary gave me on my eighth birthday in 1932 and which is still in everyday use, gives the following definition; "black, no ... particle of soot."
(8)Mary and Joe were Unitarians.